Butterfly Blessings

BOOKS BY THE SAME AUTHOR

BUTTERFLY WISDOM,
Gifts from the Dying

DARE TO DREAM:
A Survival Guide for Self-Publishers

Butterfly Blessings

A Little Book About Dying

Claire Scott

Scott, Claire, 1941-
    Butterfly blessings: a little book about dying

ISBN 0-9685416-0-7

    1. Death--Psychological aspects. I. Title

BD444.S396 1999   155.9'37   C99-900667-3

Cover & interior designed by Darlene Leger

Reprint modifications by Sherri Pilon

Printed in Canada by Friesens

FIRST EDITION 1999. REPRINTED 2001

SECOND EDITION 2004

CREDITS:

Buscaglia, Leo: *LOVING EACH OTHER*, SLACK Incorporated,
    New Jersey, 1984
Cousins, Norman: *THE WORDS OF ALBERT SCHWEITZER*,
    New Market Press, New York, 1984
Gibran, Kahlil: *THE PROPHET*, Albert A. Knopf, New York, 1984
Salzberg, Sharon: *A HEART AS WIDE AS THE WORLD*, Shambhala Publications, Inc.,
    Boston, 1997

NOTE: *The experiences described herein have occurred in various geographical settings: hospital, home care, and hospice. The people portrayed in this book are composites drawn from real events and do no depict the experiences of any one person. Names have been changed to protect the privacy of those concerned.*

Butterfly Blessings
Box 574, 7620 Elbow Drive S.W.
Calgary, Alberta, Canada T2V IK2
www.clairescott.com

In loving memory of my parents

Allan and Mary Boyd

$\mathcal{A}$cknowledgements

$\mathcal{I}$ thank my partner, Gerry for his unwavering support and encouragement.

I thank my children, Susan, Nancy and Graham for believing in me.

I thank my editor and desktop publisher, Darlene Leger in whose capable hands my hand-written manuscripts and surgical tape were transformed into work that became more than I envisioned.

And, I thank the countless "butterflies", their loved ones and my colleagues for opening up a world of possibilities.

How can death be overcome? By regarding, in moments of deepest concentration, our lives and those who are part of our lives as though we already had lost them in death, only to receive them back for a little while.

Albert Schweitzer
1875-1965

Contents

Preface

*D*uring the past 11 years as a palliative care nurse, it has been my pleasure and privilege to be present with hundreds of individuals during the course of their deaths in hospital, hospice, and at home.

Some have touched my heart and brought me to tears. Others have raised my spirits and shifted my priorities. All have given me a heightened sense of my own mortality as well as profound gratitude for each day and the opportunity it brings. To accompany such a variety of souls and walk awhile with them has been the journey of a lifetime. Courage, fear, anger, humour, dignity, theirs and mine, for each person is my mirror. I know that not one individual has been frivolously placed nor have my lessons occurred by chance.

Now and then, golden summer days offer rare moments when butterflies drift by and touch us with their unique beauty. Like these extraordinary creatures, some remarkable souls have paused briefly on their journey Home, to offer me the gift of themselves. They have enriched my life in ways that I would not have dreamed possible.

For most of us, our lives are often marked by disappointment in ourselves, frustration with others, and dreams and expectations that remain largely unfulfilled. Dying, a time when fear, loneliness and confusion catapult us into unknown territory, is no exception. However, transition from this life can wear many faces, and I am convinced that each person's journey also holds immeasurable promise.

In this little book, I offer my observations and reflections, in light and in love, in sadness and in wonder, as openly and honestly as I can. There is no Big Truth, only my truth. No answers, just lots of questions. Being human is often synonymous with pain and suffering. My hope is that by sharing my experiences, we can all grow a little closer, and become more forgiving of ourselves and our fellow travellers.

One
New Beginnings

*I*t was 1988, and I had survived a 2-year "keep-up-or-pull-over" nursing program at MRC in Calgary, Alberta. Although there had been a few more mature classmates, I definitely felt like the world's oldest living nursing student! The program's relentless pace plus the obvious demise of a 13-year common-law relationship had taken their toll: I was sad-happy, bone-weary, and grateful both were over.

Where to go for Summer Internship? The final two months before graduation were to be spent in an area of our choosing: Emergency Room, Medical/Surgical, Pediatrics, Labour & Delivery, Neonatal, Palliative Care...Palliative Care? The words jumped off the page. Care of the Dying—certainly not a choosing in hot demand. Something about it drew me closer and I knew it was right. It just *felt* right.

The year I received my nursing diploma was the year I turned 47, the year my 22-year old daughter was widowed, and the year I first saw someone die. My recollections of that event are fragmented: filmy eyes with a faraway look, the long wait for the next breath to come, an incredible stillness when it didn't—and pure physical relief when it was over. I also remember thinking we should have done more, and that none of us were really in charge. Something profound had just happened that was at the same time simple yet complex, joyful yet sad, and both involved and excluded me. What I didn't know was that my life, and the way I lived it, had been changed forever.

Changes occurred very slowly. Gradually, I felt myself touched by the frequent deaths on our nursing unit. It was something more than the impact of dying on the world around me; it was the process, the sameness, and the common threads weaving it all together.

My life had been changed forever

Whether the patient was young or old, an atheist or religious, peaceful or struggling, always I noticed:

- A light diminishing in their eyes.
- A *fullness* present in the rooms.
- A subtle distancing from the world around them.
- A sensation of time being suspended; and
- That *my* role was as an observer, a witness only; the work of dying was *theirs*.

14

Over and over, different patients in different circumstances, but the similarities became more and more apparent. There was so much to learn, in caring for people, both physically and spiritually. Oftentimes, it seemed a muddle. Where *were* these souls when they were *away*? What made the rooms feel full? How might we account for the light? Questions. Questions. And possible answers seemed to provoke more questions.

Through the years, my own spiritual quest had taken some twists and turns. Having survived a Catholic education and a brief period as a nun, I slowly became pretty unconcerned about organized religion. By age 40, I was venturing into alternative territory including meditation, astrology, shamanism, and therapeutic touch. I began by curiously venturing "Out on a Limb" with Shirley Maclaine and now consider myself to be a Universal Spirit: I pray to the God of my Heart, I believe we are on this planet to be of service to others, and I know that the answer to any problem is *LOVE*.

The answer to any problem is LOVE

As I pursue my passion for world travel, I am equally comfortable with all religions including Islam, Judaism, Christianity, Animism, and Buddhism. I believe that far more critical to the progress of our immortal souls than any doctrine or dogma is the relationship we can have with our God.

Somewhere along the way, amidst growing numbers of deaths, I felt a soft stirring, something intangible, beyond the event itself. Then, the questions:

What could this mean to me? *For* me? This is *their* journey, *their* struggle, *their* pain. But could it somehow also be mine? Could *their* stuff, in some way, be *my* stuff?

Slowly, a patient's unspoken fear became my fear: "What am I afraid of?"
(*What might happen if I take that job?*)

Their anger reflected my anger: "It's not fair!"
(*Why won't so-and-so take me seriously?*)

Their difficulty in surrendering said: "Why can't I trust?"
(*Do I always need to know the outcome?*)

Relationships with patients, their families and my colleagues began to act as a mirror, and gradually a 3-part process emerged:

1. Awareness: One by one, issues were planted right smack in my face. In trying to identify with particular people or situations, I suddenly became much more aware of "my stuff." I would barely form a question in my mind and difficulties regarding forgiveness, control, and intolerance immediately confronted me. Soon I became uncomfortable in my comfort zone.

2. Perspective: As I began to examine my own motives and feelings more closely, I sensed a shift in my understanding. What was once *your* problem became *mine*, and then *ours*. I tried to look at things from a new angle, in a different light, from the other guy's point of view. The result was that I began to adjust my expectations, pause before jumping to conclusions, and learn to accept and allow. Slowly, it dawned on me that everything was always just as it should be, though my limited view often got in the way.

3. Roles: As my awareness heightened, and my perspectives shifted, one thing became clear: when the student is ready, the teacher appears. I've known the reverse to be equally true: as often as I learn, I am also the teacher. These roles continue to switch back and forth, in the wink of an eye, even in a single relationship. As the years pass, I am grateful for the learning, and I honour each opportunity to teach.

The roles we accept, chosen by each of us on some level, belong to the dramas of our lives. When we're ready for the next lesson, along comes the person, situation or issue custom-designed to test us. The packaging can appear enormously confusing, and we wonder how on Earth this experience could ever benefit us. But, though we're seldom consciously aware of it, each role is offered when the Universe has moved things into place, and the learning will best enhance our growth and development as a human being.

Did this approach change the way I looked at life? Definitely. Did it make things easier? Definitely not! Ask of the mirror and it guarantees the answers will come—but they're hardly ever what we want to hear. Mirrors reflect, and what I saw was myself: *my* fear, *my* anger, *my* doubt. Issues began to hit home hard, and I was forced to accept responsibility for many situations and traits I had either created or supported. I learned that trust, forgiveness and love must begin with *me*. If not, I might wait forever for something to change.

Mirrors that challenge can also hold gifts

Interestingly, mirrors that challenge can also hold unexpected gifts. Heightened awareness, changes in perspective and assuming roles have given me both a richer, keener sense of trust in the dying process, and greater compassion for myself and those who journey with me.

Evelyn

GRATITUDE

*E*very once in awhile, someone comes along to open your heart and caress your soul. Kindness and gentleness mark their days and those around them are lucky, indeed.

I consider myself fortunate just to have known Evelyn. Pale and lovely, this 42-year old angel lit up the room with her smile. She came to our hospice in the last month of her life, dying of colon cancer. With thankfulness, she called us "The Best-Kept Secret in Calgary!" She gave herself to us and to our care, quietly secure in the knowledge that we were there for her. Evelyn's faith in the basic goodness of humanity had helped her through life's deep disappointments and personal pain. Earlier encounters with religion aside, she referred to herself simply as a "Child of God."

Evelyn was passionate about life

Evelyn was passionate about life. She loved sunrises and roses, Enya's music and long foot rubs, chocolate milkshakes, and heart-to-heart chats. But mostly, she adored her young son, cherishing the precious hours spent together in the soft glow of evening light.

Evelyn accepted her impending death and knew it wouldn't be long. Nevertheless, her physical and mental desire to stay for her child and her friends competed with her spiritual and emotional need to go. Each day there were questions:

> *"Do you think Uncle Wally's waiting for me?"*
> *"How can a 10-year old boy grow up without his mother?"*

On the evening that Evelyn lay dying in the arms of her dear friend, Marge, each breath came shallower than the one before. Her heart, under my hand, fluttered like a small bird, and I felt she was receiving all the love we could send. Then serenely, graciously, she was gone. And I knew, beyond a doubt, we had all experienced something sacred and holy.

Evelyn —*You gave me the gift of gratitude. I am blessed to have had an opportunity to care for you, and to be a part of your journey. And, I am thankful for the chance I have just to live each day.*

You taught me to trust in God, in myself, in others, and in the process of life itself.

Two

Myths & Messages

*P*alliative Care is the active, total care of patients diagnosed with a terminal illness, i.e. where the outcome is likely to be death. It is not curative but promotes physical, social, spiritual and psychological well-being. Palliative Care means, literally, care of the dying, with no more bells and whistles: no more tests, chemotheraphy, radiation or surgery, unless for *comfort*. Instead, symptoms are dealt with and nausea, pain, insomnia, depression, etc. are managed in myriad and creative ways.

Contrary to rumours, people are not left to die while at home, hospice or hospital. They are not written off as either hopeless or helpless. Palliative Care, once designated by a physician, brings into play an educated and experienced group of professionals and volunteers, from medical to social work, pharmacy to companions. All have one agenda: being there for someone who is dying, being physically available and emotionally present for patients, loved ones, and colleagues, and accepting, as a life is lived out, each person's process as being perfect for them.

Through our connections, we can learn so much about life and how to live our own differently. Dying and living: the paradox becomes the gift. We are tested by events that become opportunities in disguise if only we can look into our mirrors, gather courage and risk the necessary change. Dying people can teach us so much about clarity and compassion, about life, love and letting God, and about facing fear and finding our faith. Each person truly comes our way in flawless order, Divinely arranged, touching a particular nerve or pushing some specific button. Though it's often far from apparent at the time, it helps to keep in mind that we frequently learn the most from the events that try us the hardest. For me, new issues come along while old ones reappear; the lessons move fast, but the learning takes longer!

Dying people teach us about life

What messages do I receive?

- Dying people often don't need me as much as I need them, to care for so that I might feel validated and useful.

- Sometimes, I receive a gentle reminder to leave the work

of dying to the dying—to remember that my role is to accompany and to witness only. Being born is hard work and so is dying. It can't be done *for* us. The wisdom is knowing when to move in closer and when to give people much-needed space. Waiting quietly, saying little, being emotionally available, and listening to one's own heart helps.

🌹 To know I'd better watch my priorities. When I sense myself starting to fuss over the "small stuff," it's time to shuffle things around. Dying people with little precious life left help me sort out my *wants* from my *needs*. (What would be *really* important if I had just a week to live?)

🌹 To focus less on what happens and more on what it means. (The events in my life are not nearly as significant as what I do *with* them, and *through* them.)

What does dying look like? How does it feel? Why do dying people behave in certain ways? In my experience, dying is a truly unique phenomenon, full of paradoxes, contradictions and myths. No two people undergo precisely the same process and, just when things start to look even slightly routine, along comes someone to shatter our complacency. Sometimes the inconsistencies are surprising and the absurdities illogical, but there they are.

Patients are often heard to say:

"I want to die."

"It's time for me to go."

"I've lived long enough."

However, on experiencing an escalation in pain or nausea, or seeing sadness in the eyes of their loved ones, they muster the strength to LIVE, and stay just a little longer. *Mixed messages* often take over, generating an undercurrent of conflict. Actions become incongruent with what's said, and everyone is understandably confused. People who are dying frequently protect those who are close to them if they feel responsible for abandoning them.

Often, there is *dependence* upon physical care that battles with a fierce *emotional independence*—and a real sense, felt by the rest of us, that they are truly doing it their way. There is a distancing, and patients can become almost aloof in interacting with those around them. It seems that this can be a sure case of "nothing personal." So we just wait, and try to respect their choices.

A gradual *disinterest* in material things, even those avidly coveted and acquired, is almost always part of the process. Where once prized treasures were the topic of conversation, attachment to possessions slowly disappears.

🦉 Religious convictions frequently generate varying degrees of inner conflict, especially when one has faith in an *unforgiving God*. Fear can be palpable, overtaking any notion of Divine Love or compassion, and renders the dying person bereft of hope or peace of mind. Sending them love, silently and unconditionally, seems to bring calm when verbal reassurances fail.

🦉 Frequently, an odd *mental alertness* accompanies *physical deterioration* and patients are quite clear and lucid when one would expect greater disorientation. Many times, folks have eaten no solid food for weeks, surviving on ice chips and water. There they are, perched high in their beds, wanting to know the half-time score in this season's Grey Cup!

🦉 Dying can be *funny*, or, at least, dying people can be. Frequently displaying an odd, black humour, many individuals have a knack for cutting to the chase. For example, "I don't mind death—it's the *dying* that's killing me!" Many patients display a real wit and charm, even if they never have before. It seems when all the frills and extras in life are gone, they're able to enjoy some heavy-duty laughs at last.

As for myths, there are dozens involving death and dying. No other passage in life offers such opportunity for anxiety, apprehension, doubt and misunderstanding. Such mystery. Such forbidden territory. At the root of it all, I believe, is fear: fear of God, of loss, and of the unknown. Your fear. My fear. Our fear. To acknowledge just a few of these myths is a big step toward a deeper understanding of the dying process.

Most myths are generated by fear

COMMON MYTHS

1. *There is always pain.*

TRANSLATION: *I'm afraid of losing control.*

REALITY: Just about all pain can be successfully managed in the hands of skilled, compassionate physicians and caring, competent caregivers. Nowhere is it decreed that we should, and will, suffer physical pain. However, whether or not we've convinced ourselves that we *deserve* punishment is another matter altogether, often tied in to guilt or the Wrath of God. In my experience, folks who seem to maintain a certain grace in the midst of their circumstances manage to practice the fine art of blending personal responsibility (of the things they can change) with spiritual surrender (of the things they can't) to their God. The wisdom comes, says Alcoholics Anonymous, from "knowing the difference."

2. People lose their minds.

TRANSLATION: *I'm afraid I'll look like a fool.*

REALITY: The thought of ending our days in an incoherent stupor can be truly frightening. The fact of the matter is that, as this life winds to a close, many folks are lucid and oriented, or at worst, pleasantly confused. However, a special vagueness can be common when patients are unable, or unwilling, to reconcile either their own transition, or unsettling family dynamics. This then becomes a place to go—and just be.

3. There is always a struggle.

TRANSLATION: *I'm afraid I'll not rest.*

REALITY: This myth often becomes a self-fulfilling prophecy. If people believe they will struggle, they surely will struggle. What is the resistance? Basically it seems to arise out of conflict, or duality—"Our hearts versus our heads." How can we attain a peaceful state when inside, a war rages! (Dying persons often convey calm and tranquillity to loved ones but become angry or tearful when they leave.) The work of living continues, even when we're dying—often, especially then.

Physical discomfort always takes a back seat to emotional pain. Sometimes the torment lessens when those who are able, take stock of their lives, mend necessary fences, and begin to let go.

4. Death is darkness.

TRANSLATION: *I'm afraid of the unknown.*

REALITY: Numerous people, as they are actively dying, go not into the darkness but into the light. Some speak of seeing or feeling a light, while others reach out their arms, sometimes while dreaming, and often in the last few moments of life. Often dying persons just can't seem to relax, give up and let go. However, if prompted to "Go to the light," they will settle into a peaceful state and take their last breath in a matter of minutes. It's as if they are temporarily confused, or lost, and require direction, especially from loved ones.

Countless people go into the light

---

5. Die and you die alone.

TRANSLATION: *I'm afraid...*

REALITY: Time after time, when death is imminent (and sometimes earlier), patients will acknowledge the presence or show recognition of deceased loved ones close by. Is it the drugs? Are they disoriented? Rarely. And these events are too similar for too many people to be considered coincidences. Often lucid and alert, they will report the deceased beckoning, or waiting for them, "on the other side." Knowing they'll not make the journey alone frequently seems to bring great comfort and peace of mind.

And on go the myths. Fear-based and fear-fed, they serve only to mystify and muddy the dying process, leading to uneasiness and misinformation. How can we overcome fear? By focusing, as clearly as we can, on its opposite. Contrary to popular belief, the opposite of fear is not courage, it's love. Love held in the hearts of people dying, their loved ones and their caregivers can and will override and displace fear. There just isn't room for both. I refer to a universal, unconditional love: love of God, love of self as a *child* of God, and love of one another as brothers and sisters. Love means changing our perspective when necessary, and being willing to approach situations in a different light. It means acknowledging who and what another person is while supporting their spiritual growth. Love goes beyond tolerance and into acceptance, of each and every individual and their right to be. Though there are times we may become *dis-spirited* or lose our direction, we are all on a collective journey *back* to our Creator. Love is what makes the difference along the way.

We are each of us angels with only one wing,
And we can only fly embracing each other.

Luciano De Crescenzo

Malcolm

ACCEPTANCE

*L*est I give the impression that all cases are resolved, and all caregivers feel connected, I am moved to remember Malcolm.

Suffering from a chronic fungal pneumonia, and only 36-years old, Malcolm was admitted to a small AIDS hospice by his sister. Right from the beginning, it was clear that he was certainly less than thrilled with his situation. Malcolm resembled a bike gang member: long, straight hair, thick black beard and fierce, multicoloured tattoos. He would squint and peer sideways at us; we always wondered whether this was the day he'd strike out. But in actual fact, Malcolm was quiet, reserved and very co-operative. He neither asked for much nor gave a great deal, but his three sisters loved him like crazy. Malcolm had a passion for long, hot baths and strong black coffee, and the fact that his was the neatest bedroom in the house was always a big surprise!

Malcolm neither gave nor asked for much

Malcolm's gradual deterioration over a two-month period still didn't prepare us for the helpless, child-like man we cared for at the end. This very private person, intensely independent, lay curled up in his bed, staring, while we cleaned and changed him. However, on some level, a connection was made, and we

34

believe that he let himself trust as he invited us in, to a place where few had been able to reach.

Malcolm died peacefully one afternoon with his sisters at the bedside, softly stroking his tattooed arms.

MALCOLM —*You gave me the gift of accepting things I cannot change, knowing there is a purpose far greater than I can comprehend.*

You taught me about objective compassion and unconditional love—for the harder-to-love. You were that distant, unreachable part of ourselves that can be isolated and alone. In other words, you were us.

Three

Mary In My Heart

*I*t's one thing when the patient is a member of someone else's family, and quite another matter when the dying person belongs to you.

In April 1997, my mother, Mary, was diagnosed with advanced lung cancer. Declining all palliative surgery and treatment that might extend her life, she displayed her usual philosophical attitude. "Claire," she said, "I don't think I'll be very long." And she wasn't. She died, just six months later, in November. The period that passed between her diagnosis and her death was, for me, one of deep sorrow and unexpected obstacles, always challenging and often overwhelming.

Born in Winnipeg, Man., in 1914, and following her mother's death in childbirth, she was raised first by her ageing father, then by an adult sister. Mother attended private American schools and travelled to exotic foreign countries, long before it was popular for young ladies to do so. Her work history was fairly brief, and in 1940, she and my father, Allan, were married. The following year, war raged on, I was born, and Dad began four years of service overseas in the RCAF.

My sister, Kathy, arrived in 1944, and during the next 53 years, Mother kept very busy with children, grandchildren, and her marriage to my alcoholic father. The latter she undertook in her steadfast, no-nonsense manner, endeavouring always to instill as much constancy as possible in the lives of her children, and as much normalcy as she could in her own. Often appearing cool and reserved, Mother was a superb juggler of many lives: art gallery administrator, pianist, philosopher, armchair politician, film aficionado and world traveller. She loved a great joke, good theatre, summers at the lake, bridge with Dad, big bands, flowers, Christmas—and us.

Mother was a superb juggler of many lives

Frequently sceptical of many of my hare-brained schemes and dreams, Mother and Dad nonetheless supported nearly everything I have done. Offering encouragement and promising love, they gave me the heart to believe in my dreams and the freedom to make them fly.

"It'll be just like a pyjama party," Mother said, as I planned a leave-of-absence from work to care for her at home. Delighted at the prospect of spending her last months in her own apartment, she expressed appreciation when I offered to provide professional nursing care with a daughter's touch. It was something I dearly wanted to do, as we lived hundreds of miles apart. This made visiting tricky, especially during my Dad's illness prior to his death three years earlier. I had felt inadequate and wished I could be with him more often, and our new arrangement would balance things out for me.

But life had other plans in store for both of us, and our dreams began to unravel. All at once, Mother was moving into my sister's house, her things were divided up, and the apartment rented out. One day, she took a tumble out of bed and was admitted to hospital where she died two months later. As a way of coping, I believe, with personal losses and increasing hostility amongst family members, she quickly became quite vague, and then very confused. My flying trips, as well as offers of help, were either tolerated or simply rejected, and Mother died one night with my sister at her bedside. There was no formal service, at Mother's request.

Today, our families remain estranged.

My story isn't new nor is it unique; similar events occur frequently in my line of work. There, of course, I am sufficiently detached in order to be therapeutic; a new patient is admitted, and we must move on. This time, I was not detached, and I couldn't move on. My losses were searing: that of my dear Mother, plus one most unforeseen, my sister. Nothing had prepared me for the double whammy. Everything hurt.

Following a small memorial service with my immediate family, the questions began: Why had my mother's passing basically not included me? What could all the hostility mean? When would there be family reconciliations? In order to move from a place of bitterness and resentment (where I could stay stuck and eventually become sick), I endeavoured to sort through it.

My losses were searing

The first step, simple but far from easy, was to believe that things were just as they should be, with not one person or event out of sync. On some level, the entire play had already been written, with me as co-author. Just because I couldn't remember my lines, here and now, didn't mean it wasn't perfect for me!

The second step required that I go through the pain in order to see the opportunity. In other words, it wasn't so much what was happening but how I responded, and how I adapted to my circumstances. The only avenue was to apply the three-step process.

The Three-Step Process:

I   Awareness:

Of my feelings of anger and disappointment, of the manner in which I related the situation to others, and of actions I might later regret. I endeavoured, most of all, to be conscious of Mother's need for peace and harmony. I felt certain the whole mess represented something quite beyond what I could see as the Universe had, no doubt, worked very hard in order that we might play out this hand. Otherwise loving relationships had erupted into chaos and conflict, and the rules of the game had changed.

II   Perspective:

Involves wearing the other guy's shoes awhile, even when they pinch, they hurt, and the style and colour are all wrong. So I asked myself:

- *How would I feel, caring for a series of ailing family members?*
- *What would it be like to have an out-of-town nurse-sister, full of medical advice?*
- *How might it be if my family members were at odds?*
- *What would it mean if I were dying, and afraid?*

Once I could *feel* from another person's point of view, something shifted, and I was better able to adjust my expectations, take things slower, and accept ultimately, what I could not change. By reacting differently to the situation, new energy was breathed into it, and the direction shifted, lessening the struggle. So I put on the shoes, and prepared to learn, by assuming:

III Roles:

🌹 *Of the student:* I began to wonder if Mother knew what we didn't—that it was not in our best interests that I assume her care. Perhaps others had a greater need. Again, it came through loud and clear that we don't always get what we want. Most of all, I was being given a huge opportunity to test my tolerance, compassion and unconditional love. And of course, there was the hardest lesson of all: to learn to let my Mother go.

🌹 *Of the teacher:* I tried to suggest ways my children might cope and weather the storm. As parents, we don't have all all the answers, but age surely does confer some measure of wisdom! I was acutely aware that I was demonstrating by example and that my actions could have far-reaching effects. My relationship with Mother changed as we considered her various options together. I freed her from any commitments to me, encouraging her to do it her way. This gave me great peace and a chance to show my gratitude for all she had meant to me. I released her. She, in turn, did the same for me.

Mother and I released each other

How strange, how lonely it feels to let go of someone you love, and to contemplate the hole in your life where they used to be. Long ago, my soul had been attracted to this woman, this family, these circumstances, for the unique opportunities they offered, and I am grateful to these souls for caring enough to be part of my journey. In an instant, I went from being a daughter, and became the matriarch, the crone, and the elder. The roles changed forever, and so have I.

As Yogi Berra once said: "It's not over till it's over." Time passes, hearts heal, and I shall continue to trust in a plan far greater than I know.

TO MY MOTHER —*I miss you more than I can say. I shall hold you in my heart, as you once held me.*

John

LIVING IN THE PRESENT

*T*his wonderful 68-year old gentleman was, indeed, a gentleman: quiet, considerate and most appreciative. John's pixyish appearance and ready smile made him easy for all of us to love. Due to a stabilization of symptoms, he was a home care client for an unexpected 11 months. Not once in that time did he ever complain, even when he sometimes should have. His marital situation was special: John was loved to pieces by his ex-wife, eagerly awaiting her daily visits and homemade applesauce. And she was loved even more in return. Childless, they still had one other, and each day was a gift.

A week before he died and a 2-year battle with cancer exacted its toll, John took to his bed, deteriorating rapidly. He had espoused no particular faith, professed no definite religion. He simply lived his time on Earth in a genuine, straightforward manner, a kind and gentle soul.

John lived his life NOW

On his last night, as we held him and wished him "safe journey," I learned later, that at the same time, my mother had died, miles away, while my sister bid her the same. Mother, like John, had no belief in an afterlife. She, too, had been equally philosophical about her cancer.

JOHN — *You gave me the gift of living in the present. The yesterdays are gone and the tomorrows aren't here yet. NOW, is all we have for certain.*

You taught me that we are truly all connected. As my sister cared for Mother and we cared for John, we all became One, giving and receiving as we were able. My wish to be with Mother was granted in a different way, and, through John, I shed some long-overdue tears, and blessed them both.

Four

Caring For The Family

*S*ince all of us are born into families, and most of us seem to acquire loved ones, I would be remiss not to include the dying person's support system. Sooner or later, we will all get to deal with the death of someone we care about. Whether it's a loving, harmonious experience or "the death from Hell," it will be remembered and recounted for a long, long time. Dying is intense for patients, but can be almost unbearable for their loved ones. They are doing the best they can, at any given time, no matter how it looks to outsiders or how it seems in hindsight. I have witnessed countless occasions where the best-laid plans and the most honourable intentions just aren't working. To say that flexibility, a few nights' sleep, and a sense of humour help would be a huge understatement.

In my experience, two areas appear to trouble people the most:

1. *Fear of making mistakes.*

This leads to hurt feelings and misunderstandings, and even the strongest bonds can be tested. The uncertainty

and uneasiness around what we do or say at funerals
is often what we wrestle with before a death.

2. *Things don't happen as expected.*

Even when death has been accepted as the probable
outcome, there are times when:

- Patients don't die.
- Out-of-towners must return home.
- Medical conditions stabilize, and patients are discharged.
- Long-buried feelings erupt under stressful conditions.

We are the keepers of secrets

People working in a palliative setting, and most particularly
at a hospice, become part of the circle involving patients, loved
ones and caregivers. We listen, watch and wait; we laugh, cry, and
love. We are the keepers of secrets and the guardians of hope.

Along the way, we try to answer questions, as honestly,
yet compassionately, as we can:

1. *How much longer?*

This is definitely the most frequently-asked question.
For us to say, "within 24 hours or so," is generally about as

close as were willing or able to risk. Death truly does occur in God's good time, and the aceptance of what can't be changed seems to lessen anxiety and frustration.

2. *Do you think they can hear us?*

Yes. On some unconscious level, I believe an unresponsive person hears us. There have been instances of individuals awakening from comas only to repeat things that were said in the room. So, talk to your loved one, and say what's in your heart. There's a good chance you're being heard.

3. *Do they know we're here?*

Again, yes, on some unconscious level. Why not believe patients know they're not alone and are less fearful because of this. A touch of the hand, a whisper, a kiss. Often, it takes an effort to reach out, but it means *everything*.

4. *Why don't they sleep at night?*

- They are *afraid* to close their eyes for fear they might not wake up.
- Nights are *long*. Often there's restlessness or disorientation.
- They sleep most of the *day*!

Music, sedation, massage and warm milk are helpful, but sometimes they just need to squeeze every minute out of the time left here on Earth.

5. Why do they struggle?

Now and again, there's a component of emotional pain, torment or anguish that is unresolved. In my experience, people who have not lived life fully often fear death. The physical body cannot sustain life but the spirit tenaciously holds on. Perhaps a dread of death *is* the life unlived. Also, the perception of unfinished business, either their own or that of loved ones, can result in a reluctance to let go.

Perhaps a dread of death is the life unlived

---

6. What do they see?

At the end of life, when awareness diminishes and breathing becomes shallow, there is often a cloudy look in eyes that no longer focus. Dying persons frequently call out a name, or mistake those present for someone already deceased. Where do they go? What do they see? Glimpses perhaps, of other souls, other worlds, that welcome them, and seem to bring immense comfort. They appear connected to a peaceful place where family and old friends await.

7. What can we do to help?

Quite simply: *Just be there*. Be fully present. Really listen. Touch this person that you love. Sit in close. Cry, alone or together. Laugh. Sing a lullaby. Play music. Give a long foot rub. Read a short story. Look at photos. Eat ice cream. Give an angel pin. Watch videos. Pray together. And, as your loved ones lie dying, gently place your hand over their hearts and tell them:

- You love them.
- You will miss them in your life.
- You release them into the light.

The smallest gesture makes the biggest difference

If you can't speak the words, say them in your heart. Hearts understand. Trust whatever happens, knowing your love has given wind to their wings and sweetness to your tears. Just know that your smallest gesture makes a great big difference. Be creative. Take a chance. And be prepared to receive *butterfly blessings* all your own!

8. How will we know when it's over?

- You will wait for a breath that never comes.
- You will feel a change, a shift.
- You will experience stillness.
- You will sense a certainty inside you that a life is finished.
- You will know, somewhere deep inside, that your loved one is flying free.

9. What is a "good death?"

The importance of knowing absolutely that we are loved encompasses all religious, philosophical and spiritual paths. It is believed by many that the state in which we die impacts profoundly on our continuing journey. Thus, the manner in which the door closes here on Earth is of utmost importance when it opens to the future. My sense of a "good death," one where the dying person is able to achieve an acceptable level of peace and harmony, is that the following are included:

- Belief in a Higher Power, Supreme Being, or Creator
- A personal support system
- An understanding that their life has meant something, and that the world is left a better place for their having been here.

In fact, a good death looks a lot like a good life!

10. How will we manage when they're gone?

You won't, not for awhile. And life will never look exactly as it did before. Being kind to ourselves, crying when we need to, and connecting with our memories can ease the pain, and see us through.

11. Why do you work in palliative care?

Most people search every day to learn their purpose here on Earth and to find meaning in their lives. Relatively few are so blessed as to discover their place in the world. I am one of the lucky ones. In caring for the dying, I get back so much more than I can ever give. Not a day passes without knowing that some small thing I've said or done has made a difference. Being validated both as a nurse and as a human being, cannot be measured in terms of prestige or monetary compensation.

As dying people face their issues, I am compelled to face mine, to consider what is really important, and what isn't. They test me, check me and make me "walk my talk." They are my mirror, my truth and my liberation.

In honouring their gifts of love and courage, I feel committed to explore, to risk, and to reach out even further. More than anything, I believe my work with the terminally ill to have had the greatest impact on how I've come to view the world.

My roles have been varied: daughter, sister, wife, mother, career woman, political activist, and spiritual seeker. Whether I'm raising a family and planting a garden, or studying new languages and volunteering in West Africa, I believe all are pieces of a mosaic, held together by the glue that has been Palliative Care.

And what is it to work with love?...
It is to charge all things you fashion with
a breath of your own spirit,
And to know that all the blessed dead
are standing about you and watching.

Kahlil Gibran

Marion

Patience

*W*hat to do when you're 80 years old and have terminal lymphoma? Where to go when you've been in hospital for over four months, and you don't die?

Amidst several nasty turns and a few big scares, Marion began her fifth month in an acute-care facility. Admitted in crisis, her condition had stabilized and there she lay, very much alive. Due to episodes when her symptoms would worsen, attempts to transfer her to long-term care had failed. Marion was bright, feisty and a very funny lady.

Never in her wildest dreams (or those of her physician, her family or us) did she plan on being around so long. Each day on the nursing unit prompted a despairing:

"Why am I still here?"

"People die in two days. Look at me."

Not a bit impressed with being our longest-term patient, Marion had carved out her own little niche, actually holding court from her hospital bed. Nightly tea and crackers in her room was by invitation only, and always involved a lively round of jokes, tears, observations and complaints.

On linen changes: *"What most people need each day is a really good sheet."*

On wearing a bib: *"Bibs can be a good thing. But you should ask a lady first."*

For Marion, the days were long, and the nights even longer. Taped "golden oldies" were her favourites, and frequently the 24-hour shopping channel would lull her to sleep. As time passed, she became convinced she was a burden to her family; they spent countless hours reassuring her she wasn't. We tried various approaches to provide comfort or lift her spirits. Humour helped, sometimes. Love and support would work, but not always. We were convinced that Marion was sustained by her witty, laconic approach to life.

Marion was sustained by her witty approach to life

Marion was transferred to an extended care facility where she died peacefully six months later. Her quips and remarks were recorded in Marion's Book (where all could write), and which became a permanent record for her family.

MARION —*You gave me the gift of patience and the certain truth that we don't always get what we want. Your cheery resignation in light of ongoing disappointment made you truly special.*

You taught me about expectations and how they block the path to trust. You helped me to let go of preconceived notions and to learn to simply allow the process.

Five

Closer To Home

*W*hen patients are dying, it's not you personally. When friends pass away, again, not you. Even in the case of parents, still, not you. For me, in the spring of 1997, cancer reared its ugly head. "The Big C?" No one knew for certain.

Ultrasound?   *"Inconclusive"*
Biopsy?   *"Inconclusive"*

Investigations into a suspicious node on my thyroid gland had proven nothing. Plans for surgery were postponed while I travelled in the Middle East. Ultimately, I spent almost five months in my chaotic world of acceptance, uncertainty and worst-case scenarios. Some days I would literally define myself through work, social distractions, and the busy-ness of living. However, since there had been no definitive diagnosis, and therefore, no plan for treatment, it seemed other days just hung there, suspended in time, with no real focus.

Recounting my own advice, given over the years, I tried to be realistic. After all, as long as there was doubt, there was also hope. But, inevitably, my limits and boundaries would evaporate, and I would be left with a subtle, pervasive sense of loss. I recall thinking: "So this is what it feels like; these are the fears so much a part of each patient's journey." Although I knew all was in order, and that I was precisely where I needed to be, I didn't *like* where I was one little bit. Eventually there came the day when, weary from all my intellectualizing, and with the certainty I could go no further alone, I did the only thing left: I gave the whole matter up to God, and waited.

Mine was a frightening world of fear and loss

Surgery. Half my thyroid was removed and sent to pathology. Once again, the results were inconclusive and further testing of the section was required. The incision was closed, staples secured, and a drain attached for fluid collection. The I.V. came out, and I went home to wait. And wait. Time passed, in surreal, not-quite-here days, as I gave up trying to figure anything out, and I trusted.

Day 12, and one of the most joyous words in the English language: "Benign." Sweet release. Overwhelming relief. Pure gratitude, all running together and all *very real*. I was back from the pit and back in the game. In my own brief encounter, I had dipped just one toe into the water, and taken only a single, small step into the frightening world of grief, loss, denial and despair, and it was quite enough, for now. Exhausted but jubilant, I had a sense that, once again, there had been a shift, and something, somewhere had irrevocably changed. And, that this change would affect the way I lived my life.

Invaluable lessons emerged from this experience, lessons *best* learned by just these very circumstances. First, I believe it was necessary for me to gain a deeper understanding of the human condition. Over the years, I had known about trust, believed in love, and had preached hope. What I needed to do was *feel* all of it, so that I might then approach those in my care with greater empathy and compassion.

It was also necessary so that I might learn to receive, and accept what was offered by those around me: love and support from my partner, hope and encouragement from my children, and patience and understanding from family and friends. I found that people like myself do well to put themselves on the *other* end more often and move out of their positions of power and control. A very humbling experience.

I discovered, through this process, that my staunchest ally had been my mother. As my ordeal was ending, hers had only begun. But throughout this most painful period in my life, she generously offered me her positive outlook, her loving concern, and the gift of herself—true butterfly blessings I shall treasure the rest of my days.

On a soul level, the location of the node was a significant one. The neck and throat: what did it mean? According to Eastern philosophies, this particular energy center, or *chakra*, is related to power of the will, communication and personal expression. Blocked energy in this area sent me a huge message to get off my duff, "walk my talk," and speak (and write) my truth.

Things do happen for a reason. Every situation that challenges us can potentially be the one providing us with increased awareness, changes in perspective and unique opportunities as students and teachers. The Universe is devoted to ensuring our best interests and brings issues to our attention, gently at first. Choose not to listen and the message gets louder, urging us to accept responsibility.

Is it easy? Hardly ever? Are there choices? Always.

Choices lead to change, changes to transformation, transformation to learning, and learning to growth. The more we learn and grow, the more we are guided toward finding and fulfilling the unique purpose of our lives.

Jim

GOING DOWN INTO SORROW

*I*t's true. Things change somewhat when young people die. The dynamics around them are different: parents are losing a child, and siblings and visitors bring youth and vitality to the process. (Often, very small children whose parent is dying open up yet another layer of issues). The pain of loss felt by everyone is profound.

Jim was 27 years old. He stayed just five days at our hospice, bringing with him a lovely young sister, his lifelong friend, and his mother and father—all grappling with the terrifying reality of Jim's very rapid deterioration.

Jim generated a calm, healing energy

The camps were divided: mother and father in one, sister and friend in another. Tension and confusion reigned in an undercurrent of hostility; everyone walked softly, careful not to cross paths. As so often happens, the patient becomes "the eye of the hurricane," and Jim, though comatose, somehow generated a calm, healing energy. His death was a peaceful one with all of his loved ones around, telling him how they loved him and giving him permission to die. United briefly in their collective sorrow, each loss was palpable as they coaxed him toward the light. Then he was gone.

Later, when everyone left, I found Jim's sister sitting cross-legged on the bed, chatting to him, tears streaming down her face.

"I want to do something, but I don't know what," she sobbed.

I thought a minute. "Would you like to help me wash him? We could do it together." And we did, slowly, while she recounted stories of Jim and their childhood together. Afterward, she expressed lasting gratitude for the chance to feel useful, and for those tender, intimate moments she would treasure always.

JIM—You gave me the gift of going down into sorrow and truly feeling it. Your family managed to meet where the pain held them together. You were the loss they shared.

You taught me to keep my own counsel, to question less the failure of nations to come together in peace, and to concentrate more fully on creating harmony within myself and my circle of family and friends.

Six

One Wish...

*I*f I had one a wish it would be that each person reading this spend some time with a dying person, someone who is terminally ill. Care for a relative. Visit a friend. Volunteer in a hospice, hospital or long-term care facility. Gather up your courage, acknowledge your doubts, hold love in your heart, and trust the process. I am certain of the impact on my own life. You, too, will be richly rewarded beyond all imaginings.

So, adopt a dying person! Will you be ready? Probably not. Will you know what to expect? Rarely. But do it. Get in close and listen. Laugh. Cry. Pray. Share. Have faith, be grateful—then know you must let them go.

We are living in truly extraordinary times, each of us playing our part as humanity makes an evolutionary leap in consciousness. More and more people are discovering that the old order is failing us. We are being forced to confront *huge* problems in families, economics, education, international affairs, and our environment. As part of a paradigm shift in awareness, our challenges are unprecedented.

What will happen? Where will it take us? Great numbers of souls have already begun leaving Earth, entrusting the work of renewal to those who will carry on. The crisis is also the opportunity: our wisdom will be in replacing competition, materialism and fear with co-operation, spirituality and love. We have so much to learn from those who are dying and handing us the keys. By accepting death and living life, we have the means to open the door, to a world of limitless possibilities.

Butterflies

Ours for an instant as they vanish on a breeze,
each one our student, our teacher,
our mirror,
ourselves.

Blessings

Gifts of the Heart, of magic and of wonder,
when two souls touch,
and for one perfect, precious moment,
all things are possible.

Claire Scott

Afterword

*D*ying and death. Just what makes death such a unique opportunity, such a grand passage? Perhaps it's our chance, even our obligation, to stop awhile in another place, to *review* and *remember*.

Consider that we are born, as someone said, "terminally ill." That we are moving, our entire life, in the direction of our death, which opens the door again to our life. Just suppose that, out of our human suffering and personal pain comes an innate knowing that we are passing over and passing through, to the next phase of our journey, wherever that takes us. Just suppose we will then look back over the life we've just lived, and with deepest compassion and objective wisdom, *review* the intent behind our actions:

🐾 *How did we measure up to our own expectations?*

🐾 *Who do we owe?*

🐾 *Did we live the gift fully?*

🐾 *Where was there peace and harmony?*

🐾 *Which times did we lose, or discover, our God?*

🐾 *What would we do differently? Why?*

Just suppose, also, that death provides this backward glance so we might *remember* (re-member), or reconstruct, our lives. We would then have the opportunity to view these lives through the eyes of all those who were affected by our actions. This would allow us to feel the full impact of these actions so we might develop and adjust our own system of checks and balances.

Death allows us to review and remember

The knowledge gained from this after-life review would then be woven into the tapestry of our souls, to become who and what we *really* are. Every *action* (together with the intention behind it) would carry a certain weight, which would be counterbalanced at some point by a *re-action*. Some call this process "cause and effect," others call it *karma*. It means that everything we do has a result, and every result a corresponding action.

What if death takes us to a place where we become the judge, the judged and the process—all rolled into one?

- *What if death is the threshold, a doorway?*

- *What if the doorway acts as either an entrance or an exit, for a particular person, at a particular time?*

- *What if a closing here on Earth is actually an opening somewhere else? And vice versa?*

We are spiritual beings on a human journey. Just suppose that in order to experience life here on Earth, we would be arriving from somewhere and then leaving for somewhere, as well. If we use our *life lessons* in further circumstances that would test and nurture our spiritual growth, there would be no logical reason for limiting that lifetime to just one-to-a-customer. Ultimately via "cause and effect," we then assume much greater responsibility for our thoughts and actions along the way. What if we could see, feel and realize *fully* our lives as we have designed them: *ourselves!*

What if:

- *We are born to die, and that we die to be reborn.*
- *Together with our God, we co-design the blueprint of our lives.*
- *We have free will and can alter the blueprint.*
- *We know before we're born, and we remember when we die.*
- *We are created children of God, thereby all becoming brothers and sisters in Spirit.*
- *As brothers and sisters, we are fundamentally responsible for one another's welfare.*
- *What affects one family member affects the whole family.*
- *Language or rituals make no difference— what does matter is our trust in, and love of, the God of our Hearts.*

🐦 *Love of ourselves and love for one another are God's gifts.*

🐦 *God is Home; we are all just travellers on the long journey back.*

If these were possible, how would you live your life differently?

What would be important to you *right now*?

Who would hear that you love them?

What would you do more of?

What would you get rid of?

What do you want your own death to be like?

How do you need to live *now* in order for that to happen?

The choices that we make in each and every moment determine the course of our lives. One day when we are leaving our life behind, and we find ourselves glancing backward, how would our current choices look to us? Do we need to take even the smallest step today to change the direction in which we are going?

Be courageous. Be compassionate. Be connected, to others and to life. Sharon Salzberg teaches that "we are all intricately involved with one another, whether we realize it or not."

To understand this "is about the realization that whatever each one of us does matters." We create our own reality with every choice we make and what touches one of us, touches us all. It is said that when someone sneezes in Peking, a daisy dies in Arkansas.

Choose wisely.

Contact Information

Claire Scott would very much enjoy hearing from readers with any comments or stories of their own. Submissions may be included in a possible future book.

To contact Claire Scott regarding submitted material or to arrange personal appearances for your group or organization, please direct all enquiries to:

BUTTERFLY BLESSINGS

Box 574, 7620 Elbow Dr. S.W.
Calgary, AB Canada T2V 1K2
Fax/Phone: (403) 640-7312
E-mail: bblessings@hotmail.com

Visit our website: www.clairescott.com